The Lie Is Not Your Friend

The Lie Lies

by Marcell Smith

· Chicago ·

The Lie Is Not Your Friend
The Lie Lies
by Marcell Smith

Published by
Joshua Tree Publishing
• Chicago •
JoshuaTreePublishing.com

All rights reserved. No part of this book may be reproduced or transmitted in any form or by any means, electronic or mechanical, including information storage and retrieval system without written permission from the publisher, except by a reviewer who may quote brief passages in a review.

13-Digit ISBN: 978-1-941049-23-5

Copyright © 2021. Marcell Smith All Rights Reserved.

Marcell Smith is also the author of:
METHAMORPH Life In Poetic Meter.

Disclaimer:
This book is designed to provide information about the subject matter covered. The opinions and information expressed in this book are those of the author, not the publisher. Every effort has been made to make this book as complete and as accurate as possible. However, there may be mistakes both typographical and in content. Therefore, this text should be used only as a general guide and not as the ultimate source of information. The author and publisher of this book shall have neither liability nor responsibility to any person or entity with respect to any loss or damage caused or alleged to be caused directly or indirectly by the information contained in this book.

Printed in the United States of America

Dedication

This book is dedicated to Professor Walter Williams.
The person who started me on the correct path of realizing
the truth of who I am and from whence I came.
The formulation of the ideas expressed within are a
direct result of his many efforts to explain to me the
concept of animation as it is exercised in the daily life of us all.

Table of Contents

Dedication	3
Foreword	7
Introduction	9
The Lie Is Not Your Friend	10
Truth Is	12
Village Idiot	14
Love Tree	16
Listen	18
Love Song	20
Love Me	22
No Telling	24
Convincing	26
Golden Silence	28
General Story	30
Hero	32
Other Men	34
Ignorance	36
Just F*cking	38
A Romantic Interlude	40
Player	42
Red Light	44
Shut Your Mouth	46
There Was A Time	48
Supreme Being	50
Hands	52

Foreword

Animation above and beyond the cartoons

The writings here within, were inspired via the teachings of the unsung hero Professor Walter Williams. This individual is responsible for the freeing of many of minds, including mine. You may be yet to have heard of him; however, to think of him is to be reminiscent of the words attributed to Sojourner Truth: "I freed a thousand slaves. I could have freed a thousand more, if they only knew they was slaves."

Personal freedom is the product of liberating thoughts i.e. Truth. Thoughts govern behavior. All Lies enslave. All Truth liberates. The liberation of the mind revealed by the above quote is a liberation founded on Truth. To have accurate information is to have Truth, sometime called fact.

"Facts are stronger than argument, more profound than reasoning, more dependable than opinion, silence dispute, supersedes predictions, and facts always end the argument." * Facts, Truth, and Origin are inseparable of each other. They may in fact, be different names for the same thing. One thing to keep in mind when pursuing fact, is that there are solutions for problems, but, if you intend to live well and in the real world rather than in the world of illusion and animation, you must learn to live with Facts, Truth, and Origin.

In this particular lesson spoken of here, the question was put to me; do you know of illusion and animation? Yes, you mean like Popeye and Speed Racer cartoons, was my reply. No was his reply, I mean when you as a living human being see an inanimate object as a living, moving entity, with mind and will of its own. I mean when, you use the gift of human choice to see the inanimate as animated. The animation of importance here, all happens in the mind.

When it was made clear to my understanding that I too had been just as much involved in using my gift of human choice to make myself see the inanimate as animated, I decided to make a change. I developed the following method to do so. Drop everything you think you know. Uphold zero thought of the is, or the isn't. What is left standing is that which can stand on its own, and has zero need of your support. Only the Truth stands on its own, and has zero need of your or any other support.

See the Truth, Know the Truth, Be the Truth.

*W. Williams *Historical Origin of Islam*

Introduction

This book, a story told in the real is an acknowledgment of the only two concepts the human mind can comprehend. The human mind understands by way of opposites; it is what ever it is—either this or that. We can conceive of up because we can conceive of down, off because there is an on, left because there is a right, and so on. All other concepts will find themselves somewhere in between and therefore its comprehension relies on these opposites.

Of the many names or words used to denote the pair of opposites being considered at any giving time, the pair which has the most impact at any giving time is the Truth/Lie pair. Unlike any other pair in our sphere of comprehension, one side of this pair is real and the other is a fake. The crucial deciding factor for our well being is always which of this pair is seen as which.

Thoughts govern behavior. How we will behave, what we will think, do, feel, or say, in any situation of our day to day is determined by what and how we see the Truth/Lie pair. I present this Truth/Lie pair this way because, either consciously or unconsciously, the opposite side of the concept is always automatically comprehended whenever one side of the pair is considered. It is so in your mind because you think it so. It is so outside your mind because it is the Truth.

Truth always has and always will stand on its own. The Lie always has and always will need you to sustain it. The way to know Truth from Lie is to drop everything you think you know. What is left standing is Truth.

It is said that the truth hurts. The fact is that the Truth won't hurt you and the Lie can't.

It is so good of you to accompany me on this journey.
Thank you.

The Lie Is Not Your Friend

This time nice and slow
Say it again
The Lie is not your friend
This you need to know
The Lie Lies

To all who listen
To the made as well as the maker
To the giver as well as the taker
To all the hers and hims

Free yourself from the tyranny
That is The Lie
The Lie is not your friend

This everyone knows
Who've took the time
Discovered the vine
From which the Lie grows

Can you imagine a day
Come what may
That you completely stay
your hands reach for the Lie

Is there a place
That you might face
Where you see the Lie
To be a complete and utter waste

There is such a thing as Truth
A way that things actually are
One beginning and an end
To see or say other is to pretend

Free yourself from the tyranny
That is The Lie
The Lie is not your friend

It treats you no different than another
It coos and croons
draw you near call you dear

Tell you it will make you sound
Like you know what you haven't learned
Look like you own what you haven't earned

They say that the Lie is
Just as good as the Truth
As long as you can get someone to believe
it

The Lie leaves you looking
Foolish every again you invest and depend
On this nothing

The trinket you receive in exchange
For your Lie
Dazzle your eye and you never spy

That you just bought belief in the Lie
To believe in the Lie is to believe in nothing
Believe you deserve something for nothing

You self-delude abuse confuse misuse and
In the end you find it impossible to comprehend that
Truth Works

Free yourself from the tyranny
That is The Lie

The Lie is not your friend

Truth Is

Truth is and I am
Truth is all there is
Truth is what is Truth is
Truth is never wrong
Truth will never abandon you
Disappoint
Or fail to support you

Truth is the way out of the
Darkness of doubt
Truth is sacrosanct
Truth puts end to the lie
That you ain't

Pretty enough
Witty enough
Skinny enough
Wise enough
Strong enough

That you ain't
Got the right
Family relation
Education
Socialization
Justification

Truth is your rescue and salvation
Truth is the bearer of gifts you
Need never beware of
Truth is answer to your question

Truth is your connection to from
Everlasting to everlasting
Truth is your ever-patient educator
And suite of shining armor
Truth reveals all mysteries

I think therefore I am
I am therefore I am Truth
Truth is all there is
All that is is Truth
All that ain't is the lie

Village Idiot

It takes a village to raise an idiot

One family couldn't do it
Wouldn't peruse it
As a single entity

To do such is way
Too much work
For way too little pay

Most people aren't
Born in the idiot way

So the village give resistance to
A single family's insistence
For common sense
To have a little say in all this
And the family
Is raised by the village

Rather then the village
Be raised by the family

Love Tree

A tree of love walks to
The thud smack beat of its fruit
Hitting the ground or
Land in out stretched hand

A self-sufficient tree once planted
By the water of river
Now stand and deliver
In barren land
Casting shade and safety

Over even those who in misery
Stuff their mouth with sand
Rather than eat from this tree

Those who see foes as friends
Love as the enemy
Tolerate stumbling this tree's
Root but disdain its fruit

What a fine fix for this tree
That love can only love
It can never know of

Neglect or rejection
A lack of fun or consider others better than some

This tree just loves on and on

Listen

Listening to the call of the wild
I found it bestial and
exhilarating
The wind howled and moaned
like it
Had never been a friend to
anyone

Like it had something far worst
than the blues
like the greens
or some other unintelligible
things

I listened till the thrill was gone

Listening to the song
of angles
I found it stupendously
liberating
I dreamed a grace prolonged

Listening to the moans
Of angst and ecstasy of
humanity
I hasten to disbelieve my ear
I question for many a year
What to do with what I hear

I know
I'll sing a song or write a poem
Find a way to say all I know
Every where I go

No
That could be annoying

Listening to words of the sage
I was amazed
at how much they could talk
I decided to walk

Listening to the jest of the jester
I found the appeal of the
humorous
Is no way to be taken as serious

Listening to the complexities of
the commoner
I found that more than ever

I hasten to disbelieve my ear
I question for many a year
What to do with what I hear

Love Song

Listening to your latest recording
Sound quite familiar to me

Something from long ago

I can't quite place the space or the face I was living in

Maybe I was imagining the sound to be something I know

A whisper of recall tell it all

That sound was my pride before the fall

You sing like somebody in love
Unmistakenly there is that smile in face

You sing like somebody in love
Undeniably your vibe has that trace

You sing like somebody in love
You remind me of myself long ago

I was anticipating kind of relating to your sound

I was looking for the new

But you sing like then is now like revival is true

Like I never left the mind where my world is fine

You sing like somebody in love
Unmistakenly there is that smile in face

You sing like somebody in love
Undeniably your vibe leaves a trace

You sing like somebody in love
You remind me of myself long ago

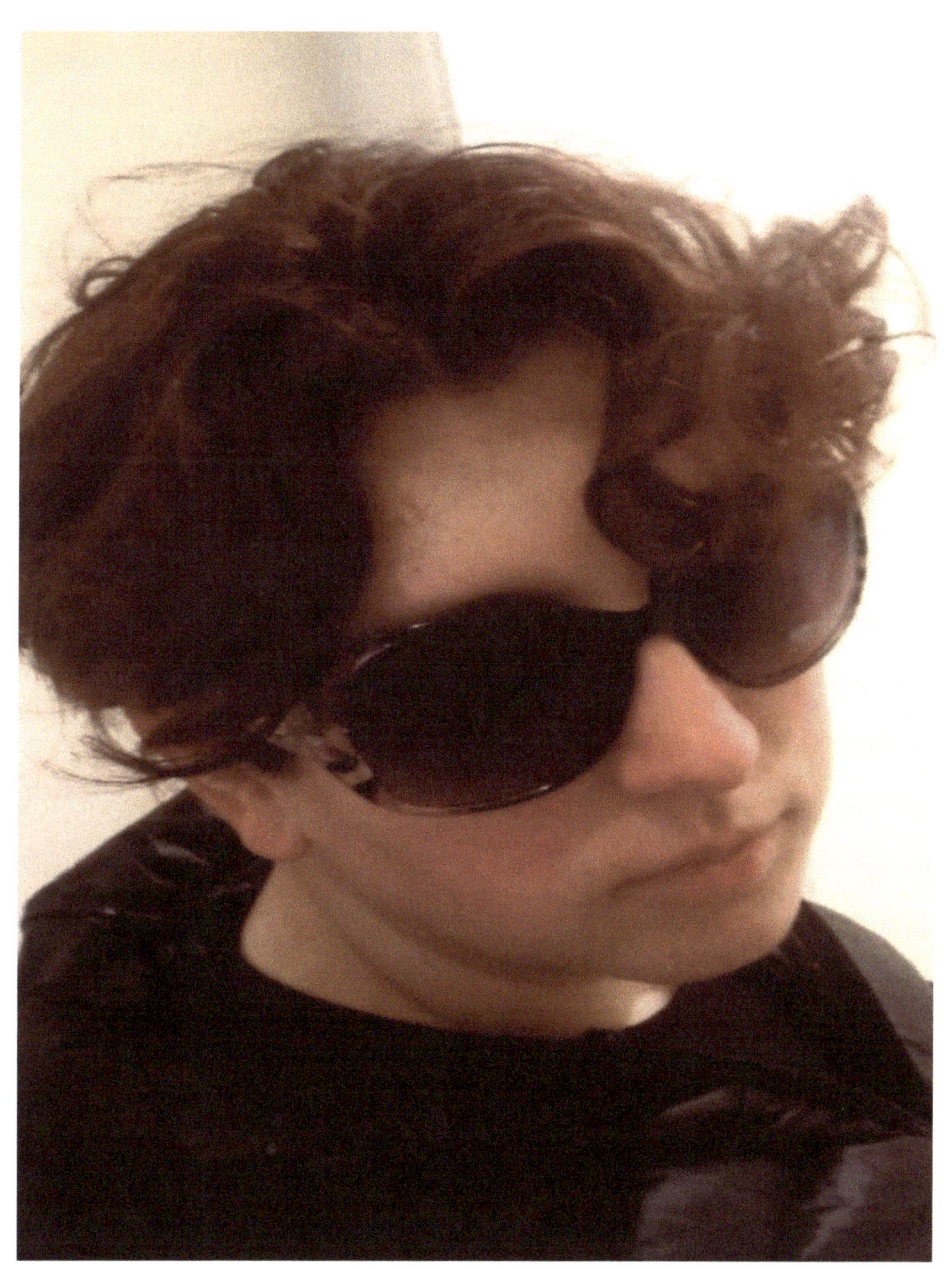

Love Me

Can't contain me
so you blame me and name me
say I was Satan sent
a malcontent
hell bound and my sound
is Lucifer lent
raised me up where they kick you
when they get you down
fools get no play
they be kissing ground
it was you who told me
if you hope
to be living large
than pitch that dope
when I said no
you say than get a gat and a crew
and go rob that store
either that or pimp that ho
I didn't come to play
I came to
claim the prize
If you be wise

give me some love

wake up fool your life is happening now
you are missing it
while you sit
holding down a corner
trading golden time
for a nickels or a dime
you be wanting game like this
it's a dame shame
trying to fine it in cocaine
and getting dissed
by that cold heart white miss
she be drop kicking fools poor or rich
quick like a gat or hard like a fist
fools swear they ghetto slick
but they getting played
just like a trick
fools talking game
they heard other fools slang
but they aint never been off the block
cept when the state had em
under key and lock
when I was banging
5 /0 say they
got a bunk down state
with my number on it
now I'm sanging
and they can all
lick on this
they thought they had me jammed up
hell I thought it too
but they let a fool
wake it up
shake it up

kicking down walls
like Too Live Crew

give me some love

Pretty ladies if you can't
work that thang
then what you doing with it
let me work it
like it's
more than just a place for your thighs to meet
I serve you up so tight
you scream like James Brown
then I say how you like me now

give me some love

No Telling

So she tell me she would tell me where love go when you can see it No Mo
Especially when you can see it No Mo

So she tell me she would tell me Where magic went when mystery is spent
Such things she tell me she know

So she tell me she will tell me Latter
When I can make her know
That I really have a need to know

I say No telling

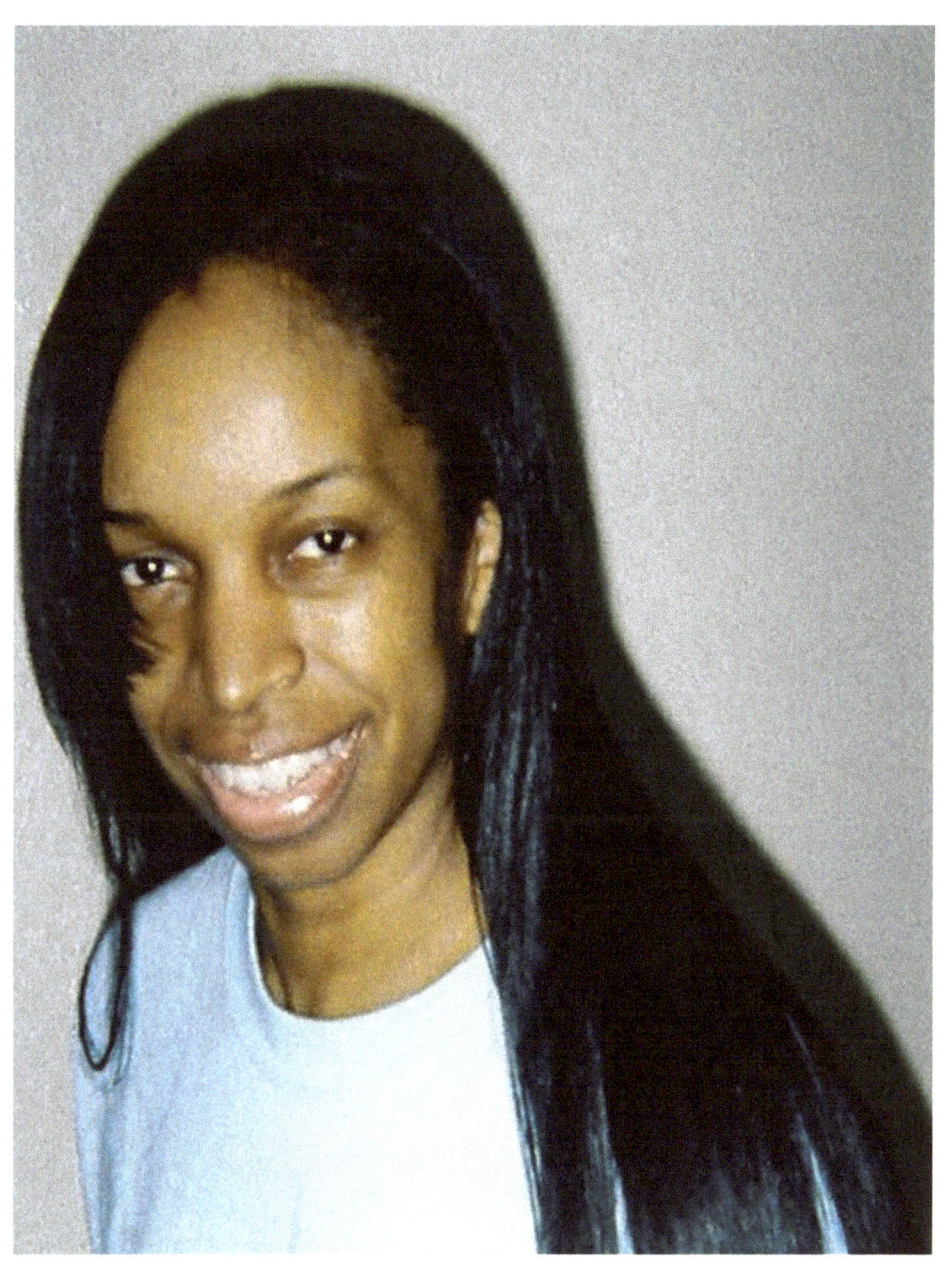

Convincing

If you can convince One
You can convince another

If you can convince another
You can convince at lease Ten others

If you can convince
Ten others
You can convince a Hundred Sisters and Brothers

If you can convince
The Sisters and Brothers
You can convince a Thousand
Dads and Mothers

If you can convince a Thousand Dads and Mothers
Ten thousand
Will convince their self

Convince the right One
Before anyone else

If you are yet to convince Another
You are yet to convince Yourself

Golden Silence

A lot of communication gets lost in the Words
Double meaning Words
Veiled hazy Words
Excessive Words
Misused Words

The meaning of Words lost
In the speaker's wordiness
Generate unrest and perturb at best

A lot of confusion is configured in the Words
Spoon fed Ill chosen Words
Fighting Words
Hot button Words
Well intentioned Words

Words used because
Because they were coming
Out your mouth
Before you thought about the
Words coming out your mouth

A lot of mixed massages transport
Through the Words
Did you instruct
To stop or go instead
Asking questions bring more Words
Down on my head
Sometime silence is golden

General Story

On the eve of this army's
crucial engagement

Grand General called his
Captains Majors Colonels
Lieutenants and Sergeants

He put a question
forward can one over come
a foe believed to be
superior

Sir No Sir quick Lieutenant
spoke in clear military

The Grand General next
question
How can one know a foe to
be inferior

Near-by Major spoke with
confidence and fervor
Sir by overcoming it Sir

Grand General's eyes took
on a tone of resolve
as disciplined and erect as
he held his body

The pursuing pause
seemed to take place
outside of time

No one knew if it was a
short or forever pause
However at its end all were
silent because there was just
one word left to say

Grand General spoke
in that long enounce every
syllable way
that military use to indicate
finality
Dismissed
And the talking was over

Hero

Mom oh mom I so wished
To be your Hero
I know I brought

A stress to your mind
From time to time
You worried about
Me in my wanderings
About

I'm sure the confused logic
I consumed as I perused my way
To be your Hero
Gave little clue
To what I was about

Neither the man you loved nor
The man you married
Ever came near figuring the plot
How to play to your Lady Guinevere Sir Lancelot
And be your Hero

So it seemed to me it fell to show
What every woman need to know
That she deservers a Hero

I took longer than you could wait
So with you my chance
To be your Hero slipped off my plate
Mom oh mom I really needed to be your Hero

At last I wonder if you needed it of me
As much as I needed to be your Hero

Other Men

In other men wars you
learned to fight and kill
other men like you

One day other men decided
this war to be over
So now what is left for you

Well for sure there are other
men who
In other men wars learned
to fight and kill other men
like you

Maybe the wars are less over
than you thought

In working for other men
you learned to embrace the
laws of supply and demand
place profit ahead of loss
and the cost
of labor fall most on the
laborer

Maybe the captains of
industry are poorer
than you thought

In pandering to other men
delights you learned to
admire the playboy bunny

See a serious woman as
something funny and the
words equal women right as
cause to fight

Maybe other men are a lot
lonelier than you thought

Once a woman said to me
hear this if you never hear
anything else

You will never reach your
potential until you are
working for yourself

Ignorance

It is a fact that a contingency
Of the population
Take strong reservation to

The Creator's stipulation to
give people
Free Will all willy neily like that

What say you then What say you

It is in their voice
The determination to fix The Creator's Mistake and
Make only the chosen few
Need be bothered
With Free Will or Choice

What say you then What say you

It is true that in ignorance some people find bliss
It is also true that others
Never miss a chance to take advantage of this

What say you then What say you

It is domination that some seek
A superiority some intend to keep
It is equality that some grade as an Incomplete

What say you then What say you

It is a lament to some
It is to others a cause to rejoice however
It is a fact that nothing supersedes Human Choice

What say you then What say you

Just F*cking

Genital manipulations absent expectations
Of revelations of Love
Truth Sex or Self

Preference sleep to being awake
Being on your seat to being on your feet
If you ain't living fine that's cause
You got something else on your mind

It ain't mama's or the man's fault
It's the lie you bought
All the Truths you left un-sought
All the fights you left un-fought

A lot of want to and a very little do of
What you say you want to
The labors of your muscle and mind
Show-up in syncopated timing
Will tell on you if you're lying
This truth never fades
If you do the work you get paid
In kind

Be it with your mind's
Eye
Memory imagination
Rear view trick mirror naked eye or microscopically
You are looking at what you see

So I question
You looking because it's significant
Or is it significant because
You're looking
To see this is to ignore that
Save when in fact
All is seen as one

What you looking at
Big breasts regrets some fearful test

Leaderless followers make way
Heralding the charlatan of the day
Tinkling syllables wrinkling into words of love
That I can't stand to hear
Because they beckon for another

Shouldna trusted that mother

But then there was the insistence

Anyway we just f*cking

A Romantic Interlude

Ronda Silverstine slick like
pond slime
And just as much infectious

She didn't just happen into your
day Slick Will
You proclaimed the game

Said any would be insane
To try against me
your luck and skill

Ronda never just kinda
do a thing
She play till her man he dance
like a monkey on a string
And she say dance monkey
dance

Slick Willy smile because to him
Every one else is silly
All the girls and the boys are
just his toys
So he laugh at chance and
romance

Destiny set the date of this
battle royal
For this match made in
purgatory
Giving others the worry
to bet with heart or mind

Ronda Silverstine
Put Willy behind first
With a move that coaxed the air
to hold her skit
Just below her business space
And then let it float gently back
to place

Slick Will didn't guess
That he was already up to his face
into the contest

Slick Will's reply to her marvel
of leg and thigh
Without hesitation
Came from a space
Like what made Motown
Temptations

He sang directly to his own beat
I didn't know it that I could
sing from the heart
Till I sign from the heart for
you

3 times he sang this
Each time he sang
It meant more to the body and
brain

His tone was lush The crowd
Went hush
Ronda was flushed and she
walked away to live to continual
this contest another day

Player

Until you learn the game
The play of the game
The rules and rulers of the game

You are at the mercy of the game
The football or the hockey puck
Has zero say-so about what way

They will be kicked or slapped about
But no doubt
they lucked out
When man made them inert and stupid
You on the other hand
Were made by the source other than man
You do
You have say how you will do
This dirty game with dirty people
That you were born into
Will you be played by the game
Play the game
Overcome the game
Will you bet
On knowledge that
Man has yet
To give life to the living

Red Light

Here I lonely sit
3:17 a.m. in the morning
The only vehicle
At this must be broken
Red light

It seem like a forever
Red light
And I think what a

Well-behaved sheep am I
Following the rules because
They be the rules

The rules they made for me

I never made rules for me
At least not rules that I follow

Maybe that is the only rule that I've made for me
Never to make rules for me
That I follow

Oops Green light

Shut Your Mouth

Shut your mouth and you will never fail
If you don't say what way
Can anyone know
what you intend to show

Failure is in the talk
Success is in what you do

You said what you said
You did what you did

But really do you claim your
Words to be gospel
Your actions to be some woe

To have befallen you
Telling you what you do

You said what you said
You did what you did

Shut your mouth and what is
Say what is
Speak and failure lives

Failure is in the talk
Success is in what you do

There Was A Time

Sometime brothers pass from brotherhood

Where together you laugh till tears
And had tears for real teary reasons

Where my fight was yours and pride was mine
Being allowed to trace your
Pace to the manhood I won

Time will lessen efforts for me
To act OK with this bitter fact

Say this is now and then was that

Sometime brothers pass from brotherhood
Into the priesthood

Choosing a different tact
Former bonds relax
Like blood's thicker than mud
Dollars make that something that was

No exception views not praising its holy name

Disciplines by threat to heave you out its game

To the world its darkness has no fame

Where value is just a state of mind and mind is all that's just

Be good priest a for the Money God
Hold high its glory
Receive the reward of your faith

All that money can't touch
Won't enter your gate

Sometime brothers pass from brotherhood

Supreme Being

Cling onto me

I love the feel of your fingers
Griped in my hair
Go where I go be where I be
Love and make love to me

With all the passion and freedom
That the courage of innocence allow

And I will feel
Less the fool
And you not think me cruel
When I do the same

Come to me
And I lay my head on your breast

Be perfectly still and let me

Find the meaning of existence
In the rhythms of your heartbeat

Hands

Hands give
Hands take
Hands up
Hand over fist
Hands feel you up
Hands heal
Hand me downs Hands shake
Give me a Hand Hands steal
How about a Hand job Hand it over
Hands handle
Hands weald
Hands hold
Hand and glove Handy man Hands Helping Hands

Photo Credits

11	The Lie Is Not Your Friend	M. Smith
13	Truth Is	Shelia Oettinger
15	Village Idiot	Krzysztof Hepner
17	Love Tree	M. Smith
19	Listen	M. Smith
21	Love Song	M. Smith
23	Love Me	M. Smith
25	No Telling	M. Smith
27	Convincing	Latrach Med Jamil
29	Golden Silence	Mitchell Luo
31	General Story	Stock
33	Hero	Stock
35	Other Men	Stock
37	Ignorance	Stock
39	Just F*cking	Stock
41	A Romantic Interlude	M. Smith
43	Player	M. Smith
45	Red Light	Stock
47	Shut Your Mouth	Jay Mantri
49	There Was A Time	M. Smith
51	Supreme Being	M. Smith
53	Hands	Stock

www.ingramcontent.com/pod-product-compliance
Lightning Source LLC
LaVergne TN
LVHW070207080526
838202LV00063B/6570